CALD
BIKING GUIDE

Pocket Rides
②

Paul Hannon

HILLSIDE

HILLSIDE
PUBLICATIONS
12 Broadlands
Shann Park
Keighley
West Yorkshire
BD20 6HX

First published 1996
2nd impression 2002

© Paul Hannon 1996

ISBN 1 870141 46 6

Illustrations
Front Cover: Above Crimsworth Dean
Back Cover: Walshaw Dean
Page 1: Lumbutts Lane
(Paul Hannon Picture Library)

Printed in Great Britain by
Carnmor Print
95-97 London Road
Preston
Lancashire
PR1 4BA

CONTENTS

SOME USEFUL ADDRESSES

Calderdale Countryside and Forestry Unit
Wellesley Park, Halifax HX2 0AY (01422-359454)

Tourist Information
1 Bridge Gate **Hebden Bridge** (01422-843831)
15 Burnley Road **Todmorden** (01422-818181)
Piece Hall **Halifax** (01422-368725)

Rochdale Canal Company
75 Dale Street, Manchester M1 2HG
(0161-236 2456)

Cyclists' Touring Club
69 Meadrow, Godalming, Surrey GU7 3HS
(01483-417217)

British Cycling Federation
National Cycling Centre, Stuart Street, Manchester M11 4DQ
(0161-2302301)

Metro (West Yorkshire trains and buses) (0113-245 7676)

South Pennines Packhorse Trails Trust
The Barn, Mankinholes, Todmorden OL14 6HR
(01706-815598)

INTRODUCTION

The Hebden Bridge area is first class biking country, boasting a splendid network of bridleways of which many have been traced, researched and drawn into this guide. Each of the rides links bridleways and country lanes, with a very minimum time spent on busier roads. A further benefit is the creation of several permissive bridleways through the efforts of Calderdale's enterprising Countryside Service. These link various bridleways and thus help create practical circular rides: some are marked on the Outdoor Leisure map. All the selected rides are based on *sensible* routes: the presence of a bridleway on the map doesn't always guarantee that it's worth using.

The countryside of the Calder Valley is an outstanding combination of woodland and pastures topped by extensive moorland, and these rides take in a remarkable variety of scenery. There is no escaping the fact that this is very hilly country: all of these routes feature uphill sections, though the more arduous sections are short lived. Ground conditions vary with the season and the weather, though most people enjoy the majority of their outings in the warmer months. Don't be surprised to find a dry July run transformed into a muddy December struggle. None of these rides, however, should involve too much slutchy work, though in some cases there may be a short spell where the only option, other than for a superhero, is to get off and push. These have been kept to an absolute minimum: if we'd come to walk, we'd have boots on!

Many of Calderdale's bridleways are centuries-old packhorse ways, once busy trade routes linking the West Riding woollen towns and the cotton towns of East Lancashire. Salt, lime and almost any article would have been carried over the hills by the trains of packhorses. The arrival of the Rochdale Canal brought about their demise, but they have left a wonderful legacy of hill tracks for us to trace. Soon eclipsed by the railway, the canal also left us an important leisure amenity. Throughout the length of the valley it contrasts emphatically with the seemingly vertical hills! While there is no general right to cycle on the towpath, the Rochdale Canal Company issues permits (current fee £6) and the towpath makes an alternative to a mile of busy road in Route 5. Although the canal is not operated by British Waterways, their leaflet *Waterways Code for Cyclists* makes useful reading. It is preferred that groups of cyclists (other than small family groups) do not use the towpath, as these can cause obstructions to other users.

The rides are in the 7-12 miles (11-19km) range, with the emphasis firmly on leisure riding rather than endurance test. Mention is sometimes made of shorter or easier options. The ratio of off-road to on-road riding is given for each run, but even the road work is almost exclusively on peaceful country lanes. Even taken at a steady pace, and savouring villages and sights en route, these runs fall into the category of a morning, afternoon or summer's evening ride: for families with younger members, I can confirm that the best part of a day might be allocated! Most pass a pub or two somewhere along the way, with other refreshment halts often available. Another useful feature is the indication of places of interest along the routes.

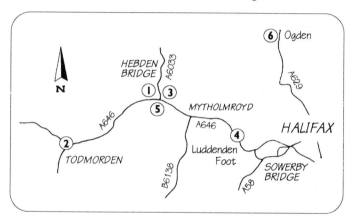

Sadly an irresponsible minority have given bikers a bad name in outdoor circles, which is unfortunate for the responsible majority. As a dedicated hillwalker, I too have had harsh words for mountain bikers carving up public footpaths in beautiful places, and have witnessed such actions in Calderdale. Bikers trundling along footpaths on the Pennine Way think their little ride can't do any damage, but the cumulative effect does cause the landscape to suffer, and with it the harassed walkers. Please take extra care not to stray from permissive bridleways, as abuse can cause our right to use them to be withdrawn.

Many people are drawn to the countryside for the first time on acquiring a bike, and often are genuinely unaware of their rights and responsibilities. Hopefully the rides in the following pages will encourage more riders to enjoy a stimulating, entirely legal journey through our countryside, leaving no lasting sign of their passage.

THE MOUNTAIN BIKE CODE OF CONDUCT

RIGHTS OF WAY

- *Bridleways* - open to cyclists, but you must give way to walkers and horse riders.

- *Byways* - Usually unsurfaced tracks open to cyclists. As well as walkers and cyclists, you may meet occasional vehicles which also have a right of access.

- *Public footpaths* - no right to cycle exists.

Look out for posts from the highway or waymarking arrows (blue for bridleways, red for byways and yellow for footpaths).

OTHER ACCESS

- *Open land* - on most upland, moorland and farmland cyclists normally have no right of access without the express permission of the landowner

- *Towpaths* - a British Waterways cycling permit is required for cyclists wishing to use their canal towpaths
  (see introductory pages for details on Rochdale Canal)

- *Pavements* - cycling is not permitted on pavements

- *Designated cycle paths* - look out for designated cycle paths or bicycle routes which may be found in urban areas, on Forestry Commission land, disused railway lines or other open spaces

OTHER INFORMATION

- Cyclists must adhere to the Highway Code. A detailed map is recommended for more adventurous trips.

THE COUNTRY CODE

- Enjoy the countryside and respect its life and work
- Guard against all risk of fire
- Fasten all gates
- Keep dogs under close control
- Keep to rights of way across farmland
- Use gates and stiles to cross fences, hedges and walls
- Leave livestock, crops and machinery alone
- Take your litter home
- Help to keep all water clean
- Protect wildlife, plants and trees
- Take special care of country roads
- Make no unnecessary noise

SAFETY

- Ensure that your bike is safe to ride and prepared for all emergencies
- You are required by law to display working lights after dark (front and rear)
- Always carry some form of identification
- Always tell someone where you are going
- Learn to apply the basic principles of first aid
- Reflective materials on your clothes or bike can save your life
- For safety on mountains refer to *Safety on Mountains,* a British Mountaineering Council publication
- Ride under control when going downhill, since this is often when serious accidents occur
- If you intend to ride fast off road it is advisable to wear a helmet
- Particular care should be taken on unstable or wet surfaces

START Hebden Bridge   grid ref. SD 991272
Start in the town centre. Car parks and railway station.

DISTANCE 11½ miles/18½km
Off road 6½ miles/10½km   **On road** 5 miles/8km

TERRAIN Virtually all the climbing is encountered within the
first mile, beyond which the route is along good tracks and farm
lanes until the unavoidable road finish from Hardcastle Crags.

ORDNANCE SURVEY MAPS
1:50,000 - Landranger 103, Blackburn & Burnley
1:25,000 - Outdoor Leisure 21, South Pennines

REFRESHMENTS
Ample in Hebden Bridge.
Pubs at Heptonstall and Widdop en route.

S Leave **Hebden Bridge** town centre by the packhorse bridge over
Hebden Water, just along Bridgegate from the Tourist Information
Centre. Across the bridge, head away and take the steep, cobbled way
on the left signposted as a footpath to Heptonstall. Known as the
Buttress, it is a historic packhorse way entirely unsuitable for motor
vehicles. Very steep indeed, it is a rare old challenge at the outset of
this trip, and when wet the setts can be particularly greasy. At the top
it joins the road by-passing Heptonstall. Turn right if wishing to do
likewise, otherwise go left a few yards and double back uphill to
resume the climb. Note the old milestone at the junction. Though
steep, this is a little gentler than the Buttress, and the old village of
Heptonstall is soon entered.

The climb through the village is on a setted road, much as it was long
ago. At the top end the modern surface returns and the climb ends.
Continue on, picking up the by-pass road and on through the scattered
settlement of Slack. Keep left at the fork in front of an imposing
Methodist chapel. Note another old milepost here. A short pull leads
through the open country of Popples Common to Colden. Shortly

after the phone box turn right along the narrow Edge Lane, which crosses the route of the Pennine Way and on past Highgate Farm, where refreshments are available.

The lane soon loses its surface and maintains a near level course to its demise. Here a farm track bears left, while the main track (a permissive bridleway) takes the gate in front onto Heptonstall Moor. The minor climb is accomplished in a couple of minutes, and from the brow the **Gorple** and **Widdop** wilderness is arrayed. Just over to the left, off route, is the historic waymarker of Reaps Cross, now sadly without its upper section. As the descent begins, Gorple Lower Reservoir appears ahead, and the liquid promise of the *Pack Horse* comes into view.

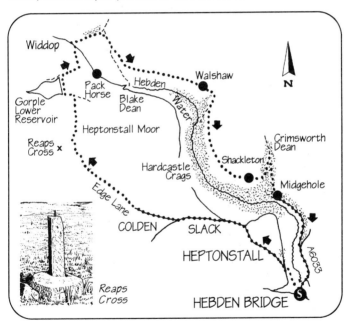

The firm track makes a sustained descent, picking up the Pennine Way again, briefly, to cross a water conduit to reach Gorple Cottages. Go left along the firm Water Authority road, which turns to cross the dam. At the end bear right for a super run down the moor (still a permissive bridleway) to join the moorland road through Widdop. Though the route goes left here, few will resist the two minute detour to the ideally

9

placed midway refreshment halt at the *Pack Horse*. Returning along the road, continue a minute further to a broad track doubling back to the right. This is the Water Authority road to the Walshaw Dean reservoirs, and is also used by the Pennine Way.

Just over a brow take the first branch right. This broad track descends, picking up an early track from the left before bearing left on the descent to a stone bridge on Alcomden Water, outflow of the reservoirs. After a short pull the track runs on above Blake Dean and along to the farming hamlet of Walshaw. This old settlement on the Saville estate includes a large shooting lodge of 1860. Keep straight on the drive out, intermittently surfaced as it reaches a fork. The right branch descends into the trees, while your upper branch maintains a level course high above the wooded valley of **Hardcastle Crags**.

The firm lane runs on to the hamlet of Shackleton before finally descending into woodland. At a junction, with the valley of Crimsworth Dean ahead, turn right. This track drops down to the National Trust's Hardcastle Crags car park at Midgehole. Continue away on the road to meet the A6033 Oxenhope-Hebden Bridge road. Turn right and descend with care back into the town centre.

ALONG THE WAY
• **Hebden Bridge** *is the self-proclaimed 'South Pennine Centre'. It is for here that most of the modern 'tourists' make, partly for its position at the foot of the famous Hebden Dale (universally Hardcastle Crags), but also for its own attractions. Its houses climb alarmingly up the steep hillsides above the meeting of the valleys, while in and near the lively centre are canal trips, a packhorse bridge, a clog factory, collectors' shops and an invaluable information centre.*
• **Gorple** *and* **Widdop** *are areas rather than places. Two reservoirs and attendant keepers' cottages uphold the Gorple name that once belonged to a solitary farm: high on the moor beneath the Lancashire border, this outpost is now but a ruin in the water gathering grounds. The brace of reservoirs appeared in 1934. There are one or two isolated farms and dwellings strung along the moorland road, but to most folk Widdop means the popular Pack Horse.This isolated inn proudly proclaims its near-thousand foot altitude, and its name leaves little doubt as to its origins.*
Widdop has its own reservoir, built in 1878 on the road to Nelson and Colne: a 5½ mile horse-drawn tramway brought materials to the site from further down the valley.

• **Hardcastle Crags** is the name by which everyone in the district knows the valley of Hebden Dale, through which flows Hebden Water. The crags themselves are in fact a modest group of rocks in the heart of the woods. The majority of this beautifully wooded, deep-cut dale is in the care of the National Trust, and attracts large crowds from far and wide. At the car park is a National Trust information caravan and often an ice cream van. Offering refreshment just across New Bridge on Hebden Water is Midgehole Working Mens Club, affectionately known as the Blue Pig.

• **Heptonstall** is a fascinating village that well merits a leisurely exploration. Steeped in history, it was of greater importance than Hebden Bridge until the arrival of the Industrial Revolution. Happily its exposed position 850ft up and defended on three sides by precipitous slopes has created a time warp in which its weather-beaten stone cottages revel. Focal point is the church-yard which separates the imposing parish church of 1854 from the shell of the old church of St. Thomas a'Becket, partly dating from the 13th century. Alongside, the old grammar school of 1772 is now a museum. Seek out the octagonal Wesleyan chapel (1764), the dungeon (1824) and the 16th century Cloth Hall. There are also two pubs, the Cross and the White Lion.

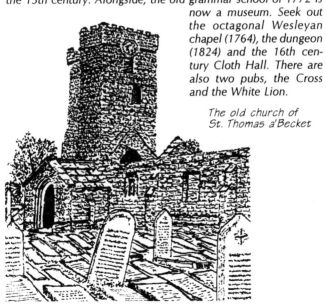

The old church of St. Thomas a'Becket

11

START Todmorden   grid ref. SD 936241
Start in the town centre. Car park and railway station.

DISTANCE 8½ miles/13½km
Off road 3 miles/5km   **On road** 5½ miles/8½km

TERRAIN Most uphill work is on two separate road climbs.
Main feature is the superb bridleway of Stony Lane.
The one rougher descent section can be avoided if desired.

ORDNANCE SURVEY MAPS
1:50,000 - Landranger 103, Blackburn & Burnley
1:25,000 - Outdoor Leisure 21, South Pennines

REFRESHMENTS
Ample in Todmorden. Pubs/village store at Cornholme
and pub at Sourhall en route.

S From **Todmorden** town centre roundabout take the Burnley road under the railway viaduct and take the first turning right along Stansfield Road. At the end it bears left round to a junction. Go left then immediately right along Stansfield Street to a T-junction. Turn right under another railway bridge, on Victoria Road. Here there is the option of a short-cut onto Stony Lane. This branches left up the road alongside the *Fountain* pub: becoming a rougher drive it climbs the increasingly steeper slope above Wickenberry Clough, winding up to level out at a junction of tracks with a lone house in front.

The more circuitous route remains on the road along to the right, soon descending over the railway to join the main road at Millwood. Go left and turn at once up Cross Stone Road. After crossing the railway this becomes a narrow lane, winding steeply up to a junction at **Cross Stone**. Keep left here up Hey Head Lane, just as far as the Todmorden golf club drive. With relief go left on here, passing the clubhouse and becoming a mere path as it runs on past a pond on the right. As it winds around the corner there are superb views over Todmorden and through the Walsden Gorge beyond to a rolling moorland skyline.

The way runs on as a broader track to the junction with the direct route at a lone house. Its broader way is taken up now as it continues straight on, rising above a wooded clough to approach the farm at East Whirlaw. Continue past its drive to a junction of tracks, and go left. The way now remains on the unsurfaced **Stony Lane** all the way to a road at the far end. In a variety of guises, the first stage is a firm surface that quickly becomes a causeyed trod across the open country of Whirlaw. It winds up beneath the scattering of rocks and heather to a gate at the end, then crosses another pasture before becoming enclosed by walls. The way now undulates along, easy going through superb surroundings to arrive at the farm at Lower Intake. A short narrow section leads onto its drive which runs out onto Shore Lane. Up to the right just before it, Mount Cross is seen standing in a field.

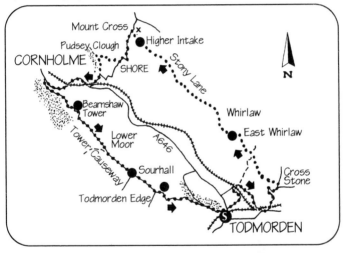

Turn left down Shore Lane, soon encountering a major hairpin. Resuming directly downhill, look out for a bridleway sign on the right. The next section is narrow and relatively rough: if so desired, simply remain on the road which is rejoined just short of the valley bottom. The bridleway is a thin but firm path dropping down to a house just below. Pass along the front and down another narrowly enclosed way: great caution is needed both for yourself and fellow users, as there is little room to pass. It is however broken up into little chunks. Firstly by following a level track along to the right, only to then leave it by turning left down another tight section to reach a lone house.

Resume downhill here to a junction, and bear right (left is footpath only) to run along to another house. Here a firm drive is joined, and this leads all the way down to rejoin Shore New Road at a hairpin. Continue down, passing under the railway to meet the main road at **Cornholme** alongside the *Waggon & Horses*.

Turn right along the road for a long half-mile, twice crossed by the railway as you go. Leave at the first opportunity, doubling back left along Carr Road just short of the whitewashed *Roebuck Inn*. This lengthy concluding road section is virtually traffic free, and runs over open moorland with more fine views, notably of the outward section on the opposite side of the valley. This runs gently on before zigzagging up past the farm at Bearnshaw Tower, with a big plantation on the right. Look back beyond Coal Clough windfarm to see Pendle Hill on the skyline.

The way eases as it climbs onto Lower Moor, and our road known as Tower Causeway eventually reaches a brow. At the T-junction at the *Sourhall Inn*, keep straight on Parkin Lane, enjoying views ahead to Stoodley Pike and Blackstone Edge beyond. The narrow road soon commences a winding descent into Todmorden, directly below, steepening near the end to descend Doghouse Lane and emerging plum in the centre.

Mount Cross, Stony Lane

ALONG THE WAY
- **Cross Stone** is a typical Calderdale hillside hamlet. *The old church, now defunct, is just on the right opposite the restaurant, formerly the Bay Horse pub. It was built in 1835 and one of many paid for, effectively, by the French in reparation for Napoleonic Wars.*
- **Stony Lane** is an old packhorse way, most of which is excellently *preserved. The lengthy flagged section on Whirlaw Common is a major highlight. Stood forlornly amidst munching sheep, Mount Cross is thought to date back to monastic times, as a waymarker on a route serving Whalley Abbey in the Ribble Valley.*
- **Cornholme** is, along with adjacent Portsmouth, the last settlement *before the Lancashire border. The valley sides are everywhere steep hereabouts as the Cliviger Gorge takes shape.*

• **Todmorden** is a fascinating little town with some outstanding buildings. Dobroyd Castle was built in the 1860s for the influential Fielden family, mill owners and local benefactors. The Town Hall was designed by their architect John Gibson in 1875 and features a group of marble figures on a pediment above tall columns. Todmorden Old Hall was built in 1603 and features a stunning frontage of gables and mullioned and transomed windows: it is currently a restaurant.

Centre Vale Park is a vast open space in the heart of town. Bought from the Fielden family in 1910 for the local population, its features include a fine statue of John Fielden MP, a war memorial garden, aviary and aquarium. The modest parish church of St. Mary's is centrally sited but tucked away, while the more outgoing Unitarian Church of 1869 boasts a tall spire.

Until a century ago Todmorden sat on the Lancashire border.

Todmorden Old Hall

START Hebden Bridge   grid ref. SD 991272
Start in the town centre. Car parks and railway station.

DISTANCE 12 miles/19km
Off road 7½ miles/12km   **On road** 4½ miles/7km

TERRAIN Despite the main climb being miraculously easy, this
is nevertheless probably the most demanding of the Calderdale
rides, largely due to a couple of rougher sections on the tops.

ORDNANCE SURVEY MAPS
1:50,000 - Landranger 103, Blackburn & Burnley
1:25,000 - Outdoor Leisure 21, South Pennines

REFRESHMENTS
Pubs at Jack Bridge and Blackshaw Head

S Leave **Hebden Bridge** town centre along the Todmorden (A646)
road, and just after the Heptonstall junction turn right on Church Lane
at Mytholm. Climb the steep road past St. James' gaunt gritstone
church, and at the first hairpin bend go straight ahead along a lane.
This quickly becomes a broad track as it enters the wooded confines
of **Colden Clough**. This same track leads unerringly on, past a few
houses to a fork. The right branch runs along to the beck, while yours
slants up to the left. Part open country takes over, and the going is
everywhere gentle. At the top of the climb the Pennine Way is crossed,
with Hebble Hole Bridge prominent just down to the right. The track
runs on, absorbing drives to emerge onto the road at Jack Bridge. The
New Delight, a very welcoming pub, is just yards down to the right.

The route however turns up to the left, and once again at the first
hairpin go straight ahead on an enclosed track, Brown Hill Lane. Keep
on to its demise at the second house reached. Take a gate on the right
immediately opposite stables, and descend the field to a bridle-gate
on a tiny stream. A reedy, sunken way heads away to a wall corner,
which required a lift over at the time of survey but should now present
an easier passage.

16

Resume on the same sunken way, curving left down to the main stream. A path rises away with the fence to a gate, from where a level track heads away. This joins a drive alongside a stand of trees, with a farm above and one below. Advance along it just to the first bend: at this track junction don't go down to the farm but take the gate in front. Head away with a wall then fence on the right, dropping down to a gate in the fence corner. A sunken way runs down from here to a bridle-gate with a large house (Land Farm nursery and garden) below. Go left above the house to join its drive, and follow this away to a drive junction in front of a bridge. Note the old square chimney on the right.

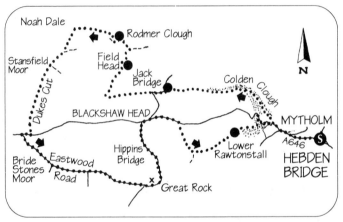

Here take the drive left to Rodmer Clough. Don't follow the drive into the house, but take the branch climbing left above its top end. After a sharp bend this forks: take the main one right, a steep, flagged way rising to level out alongside a house (Top o' th' Hill) on the left. Here our main track bears left, fully levelling out above **Noah Dale**. Ignoring any deviations keep on this, Moor Lane, becoming less firm and more moist as it runs on to end at a gate onto open moor. Advance a few yards to join a track, and go left with it. This rises part sunken alongside a fence, gradually becoming enclosed to reach a gate at the top. Just behind is the track junction known as Three Gates End.

Go right here, an easy ride now along this long track known as Dukes Cut, passing a junction at Four Gates End and keeping straight on the moor side. To the right Stansfield Moor rises to the Lancashire border at Hoof Stones Height on Black Hameldon. On passing a mast the track drops down onto a road. The quick return goes left to Blackshaw Head, but saves little. Instead go right a few yards to a junction. Note the white milestone, and the fact that the *Sportsmans Arms* is just a minute further along to the right. Now double back left along Eastwood Road. The shapely Bride Stones sit on the moor on your right.

A long easy descent ensues, ignoring any turnings off. The views to the right are breathtaking, looking over the deep wooded Calder Valley to Stoodley Pike and attendant moorland. The road descends past Staups Moor to a corner at Great Rock, well worth a break. Remain on the now generally level road to then drop to Hippins Bridge before a short pull to **Blackshaw Head**.

Turn right on the road through the village, and at an early junction in front of a chapel bear right on Badger Lane. This too provides another direct return: just stay on it to be completed within minutes. A much better conclusion leaves this road at the second group of houses on the left after leaving the village. Turn right down the firm track of Marsh Lane. Ignore turnings left and right, and with the Stoodley Pike monument ahead keep descending to reach a fork. The right branch continues down, while yours bears along to the left. This runs unfailingly on a level course past several houses. At the last the drive ends, but a clear track continues between walls. It soon reaches the hamlet of Lower Rawtonstall.

Follow the main track turning down to the right, then left as it runs on through the houses and out. It bears right at a fork in front of another house to descend into grand woodland, a smashing conclusion as it

curves down to the road. Turn downhill, taking extreme care through a remarkable series of hairpin bends. This returns to Mytholm, to conclude back on the main road.

Great Rock,
Staups Moor

ALONG THE WAY

• **Colden Clough** is a deep wooded side valley, with a couple of old mill chimneys in the bottom. In the upper reaches is Hebble Hole Bridge, where an old packhorse route crosses Colden Water. This characterful, ancient footbridge consists of two great stone slabs in a charming location. Here the Pennine and Calderdale Ways have one of their two meetings.

• **Noah Dale** is a bleak upland valley, the highest reach of the Colden Valley, in fact. One's long lasting memory is of abandoned farms, crumbling walls and unkempt pastures. Nevertheless there is a certain grandeur to this wild scene.

• **Blackshaw Head** is a windswept hilltop community astride the old road known as the Long Causeway. It stands at a meeting place of packhorse routes, notably one from Halifax via Hebden Bridge to Burnley. An old milestone stands at the fork in front of the chapel. Sadly the Shoulder of Mutton pub has closed its doors for good.

• **Hebden Bridge** is the self-proclaimed 'South Pennine Centre'. It is for here that most modern 'tourists' make, partly for its position at the foot of the famous Hebden Dale (universally Hardcastle Crags), but also for its own attractions. Its houses climb alarmingly up the steep hillsides above the meeting of the valleys, while in and near the lively centre are canal trips, a packhorse bridge, a clog factory, collectors' shops and an invaluable information centre.

The old bridge

START Luddenden Foot   grid ref. SE 037250
Start from the Luddenden junction on the main road (A646)
in the village centre. Car parking on Station Road, opposite.
Railway station at Mytholmroyd, a little under two miles.

DISTANCE 10 miles/16km
Off road 5 miles/8km   **On road** 5 miles/8km

TERRAIN A circuit of the side valley of Luddenden Dean.
The hard work is all at the start, though the surfaces are good
and the climbing is broken by gentler sections.

ORDNANCE SURVEY MAPS
1:50,000 - Landranger 104, Leeds, Bradford & Harrogate
1:25,000 - Outdoor Leisure 21, South Pennines

REFRESHMENTS
Pubs at Luddenden Foot, Wainstalls, Saltonstall and Luddenden.
Go steady if you've got to drive home afterwards!

S   From the Post office in the centre of **Luddenden Foot**, go a few
yards towards Halifax then double back up Danny Lane alongside a
large mill. This zigzags then climbs directly up to a sharp bend. Here
go left along a firm drive towards **Roebucks**. Beyond the house
continue up the rising track, which soon levels out to approach the
cluster of dwellings at Shepherd House. These include a 1746 dated
house with mullioned windows. Keep straight on the drive out, rising
a little to join a road on a hairpin bend. Turn uphill, and at an early fork
bear left off Deep Lane up Abbey Lane, a narrower, traffic free route
climbing to a multiple junction.

Go left on the main road (Workhouse Lane) which quickly levels out.
Keep straight on at a staggered junction (now as Heath Hill Road), and
as the road rises to a brow, go left on an enclosed track just after Wild
Acres. This contours the hillside, passing Oldfield Farm and along to
a junction with the main road again. Cross Stocks Lane and go just 100
yards further along the main road, then take a walled track on the right.

After a further 100 yards leave this too, by a more inviting green track on the left. This descends more steeply at the end to a road. Go left to the crossroads at the appropriately named pub, and then right. At an early fork at the *Delvers* pub, bear left for **Wainstalls**.

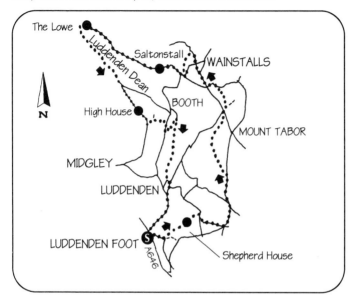

Head through the centre, past the factory, bus turning circle and down to a group of cottages. Here double back sharply left down the cobbled Kell Lane. Keep straight on this, becoming surfaced then running as a track past Tongue End and on to Wainstalls House. Continue out on the drive to join a narrow lane at a bend. Go on to a T-junction in front, then turn downhill. Ignore a branch left and continue down the dead-end road, quickly reaching the *Cat-i-th-Well* pub.

Keep straight on through Lower Saltonstall and gradually descending past Upper Saltonstall, Throstle Bower and a burial ground to eventually turn at The Lowe to bridge Luddenden Brook. This is the upper limit of the public road up **Luddenden Dean**: to the right is the Castle Carr estate. A bridleway now takes over, swinging left under the arch of the Lower Lodge and running back along the dale side as a splendid track.

This firm track runs on for a short mile, becoming fully surfaced just short of a junction with a hairpin bend. Head up the road to the right, soon levelling out before another short rise to a junction with High House Lane. Go left to commence the descent, passing the attractive High House Farm. At a terrace of houses a walled track doubles very sharply back to the left. This runs gently on, but at the first junction turn right down a steep setted way. This drops down to a couple of houses, then slants down to the left, emerging as a broad track onto the road above Booth. Turn right for half a minute then take a broad cobbled road doubling back left. This descends to a few houses, and here double back sharply right, remaining on the cobbled way. Ignore the next branch left (over the brook) and keep straight on the broad track.

This runs on to two final houses, from where the bridleway continues on into the trees. Very soon it emerges at another row of houses, Brook Terrace. At the end their drive rises left, but keep to the right branch which quickly narrows back to a bridleway. All around here are ruins of old mills. The way remains in the company of the brook to a fork just short of Luddenden church. Take the upper one to enter the centre of **Luddenden**. Go down to the left past the pub, over the bridge then keep right at a junction to drop to another bridge back over the brook. Remain on the road heading away, rising to join another road then keeping left, past Kershaw House and back to the main road at Luddenden Foot.

St. Mary's,
Luddenden

ALONG THE WAY

• **Luddenden Foot** is the little village where Luddenden Brook meets the main valley of the Calder. It was at the station here (now closed) that Branwell Bronte worked as a ticket clerk. There are two adjacent pubs, the Coach & Horses and the Weavers Arms. Today Luddenden Foot has expanded into the surrounding country with a sprawl of modern housing.

• **Roebucks** is an unsung gem dating from 1633 and featuring an unconventional layout. The roof arrangement is well seen from the track above. The widening view includes Luddenden Foot over to the left: note historic Kershaw House surviving in amongst incongruous modern development. Beyond, the Calder Valley and Luddenden Dean are divided by Midgley Moor high above its village.

• **Wainstalls** is a small hilltop village dominated by a large mill building. Of the numerous pubs attributed to it none are actually in the centre, but scattered about the surrounding countryside, as we are discovering. Though tucked away on a peaceful dead-end road, the Cat-i-th-Well inn is a popular watering hole. Its name appears an unashamed corruption of Caty Well, found on the roadside just above the pub. The little settlement of Lower Saltonstall is an ancient cluster of dark, low houses at one with their surroundings. In common with neighbouring Upper Saltonstall, it was a vaccary (cattle farm) run by the Manor of Wakefield 700 years ago.

• **Luddenden Dean** is an attractive valley, almost on the edge of Halifax yet retaining all its rural charm. The upper reaches are a curious and unjust 'no-go' area, even for walkers, as a result of one man's obsession with purchasing the area bit by bit. He then built Castle Carr, a massive 'pseudo-Gothic' Victorian castle in delightful ornamental gardens. He died before the house was completed, and its time as a home to a subsequent occupant was brief. It was abandoned, fell into neglect and finally dismantled in 1961. The only remains of note are those of the old gatehouse in the trees further up-dale from our highest point at the lodge.

• **Luddenden** is a charming village oozing with character. At the centre are pub and church. The Lord Nelson is an attractive place sporting a 1634 datestone: Branwell Bronte drank here when he was employed as ticket clerk at the now defunct Luddenden Foot railway station. Just across the tiny square a war memorial stands in front of St. Mary's parish church of 1816. Around the back an arched bridge of 1859 crosses Luddenden Brook to the cemetery.

23

START Hebden Bridge   grid ref. SD 991272
Start in the town centre. Car parks and railway station.

DISTANCE 11½ miles/18½km
Off road 5 miles/8km   **On road** 6½ miles/10½km

TERRAIN A high moorland crossing is the highlight of a ride
that visits a wealth of interesting places. The steepest climb
is a narrow road, while most of the off-road stuff is on good
tracks, including substantial sections of causeway.

ORDNANCE SURVEY MAPS
1:50,000 - Landranger 103, Blackburn & Burnley
Landranger 104, Leeds, Bradford & Harrogate
1:25,000 - Outdoor Leisure 21, South Pennines

REFRESHMENTS
Ample in Hebden Bridge.
Pubs at Lumbutts, Cragg Vale and Mytholmroyd en route.

S From the crossroads outside the Tourist Information Centre, turn along the main road for Todmorden. Escape at the first opportunity along the road at Hebble End. After crossing river and canal take the right fork for Horsehold. This narrow lane climbs unremittingly steeply: the super views over the valley are a good excuse to break journey. Out of the trees the climbing soon eases, and the road, cobbled for a section, rises through the farmyard of Horsehold and winds up to end at a crossroads with tracks. Take the level drive to the right, passing Erringden Grange and then running a splendid, endless level course. Ahead, **Stoodley Pike** monument beckons.

Passing several farms and houses, the track finally emerges onto open moor, with the monument just up ahead. While there is no cycling route to it, it is worth abandoning the bike by the wall or in a hollow to enjoy the short climb. The track, now less firm but very clear, forges on, crossing the Pennine Way and curving around beneath the monument. Known as London Road, this is a splendid section of the run, a gently curving descent all the way around the base of the moor. A wall returns for company and shepherds you for a lengthy spell along to a corner. Two walled ways head away: keep on the one straight ahead to descend quickly into **Mankinholes** (If not visiting Lumbutts turn left here, up another walled track onto a corner of the moor).

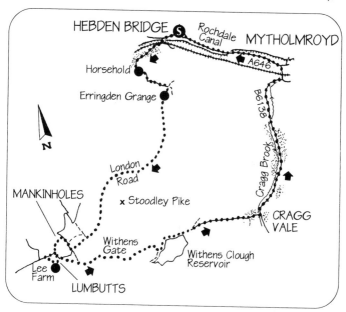

Turn right through the hamlet and on as far as a solitary house on the site of the former Mankinholes Methodist church. Here turn left down the paved Lumbutts Lane to emerge by the pub in **Lumbutts**. At the very foot of the lane an old guidepost is inscribed with 'Halifax' and 'Heptonstall' and mileages. Although you can turn left here to Lumbutts Methodist church, another tiny loop extends a little further.

Opposite the pub a little bridleway cuts down to join the road below. Go right on it a short way, rising past cottages and noting a sundial dated 1864 on a house corner. Just beyond, take a walled track on the left which runs on to Lee Farm, keeping left of the buildings. The track comes out past Lee Dam, and gives better views of the water tower overlooking Mill Dam on the left. The track turns to rejoin the road just above the hamlet. Go right a few yards to Lumbutts Methodist church, then take a walled track on the right. This part flagged way rises above Heeley Dam to a gate onto a corner of Langfield Common. The route from here to Withens Clough is a permissive bridleway. Head up the inviting wall-side causey and when the wall parts company, remain on the flagged path all the way to the moortop. Here it swings up to meet a crossroads at the mighty Long Stoop, an old guidepost of monumental stature. Go straight on, the causeyed path pointing the way to the summit of this run over **Withens Gate**. Immediately through the watershed gate is the diminutive Te Deum Stone.

Head away on the broad wall-side path beginning the descent to Withens Clough. Ahead, Withens Clough Reservoir (dating from 1894) is revealed. When the accompanying wall ends, turn left along an inviting grassy track by a crumbling old wall. When the track swings down to the right at an old gateway, the Calderdale Way branches off to the left. The permissive bridleway drops straight down to the gate below, and remains well waymarked as it passes above a small plantation. Running on to a wall corner it meets a footpath and turns right, a grassy drop down to join the hard track alongside the reservoir. Turn left to meet the road at the car park just beyond the dam. Head down the road into the hamlet of **Cragg Vale**, passing the pub and church on the left and rising to the B6138 road. Turn left along the road through Cragg Vale for a steady run into **Mytholmroyd**.

Go left along the main road for a short but busy run into Hebden Bridge. If in possession of a towpath permit (see introduction), leave the main road just after Mytholmroyd fire station by turning right up a street, Acres Villas, to gain the towpath of the **Rochdale Canal**. Part way along this meets an impasse in the form of the main road at Walkley Clogs. It must therefore be crossed to regain the towpath for the second half into Hebden Bridge.

At Withens Gate

Left:
Long Stoop

Right:
Te Deum Stone

ALONG THE WAY

• **Cragg Vale** is best known as the home of the Yorkshire Coiners. It is the most romantically recalled (though far from only) site of 18th century counterfeiting: the practice involved clipping gold from guineas to make additional, inferior coins. The sombre church of St. John the Baptist in the Wilderness dates from 1840, while the adjacent Hinchliffe Arms dispenses ale and food. Further down the main road, the Robin Hood doubles the valley's pub count. By the time we enter Cragg Vale, its bleak moorland beginnings have transformed into a deep, richly-wooded valley.

• **Mytholmroyd** is the quieter, poor relation of Hebden Bridge. It sprang up with textile mills, and large pockets of modern housing extend on both sides of the valley. St. Michael's church stands just across the river, where the valley of Cragg Vale joins the Calder. Such is the reputation of the local dock leaves that Mytholmroyd is home of a restored tradition, the World Dock Pudding Championship.

• **The Rochdale Canal** was completed in 1804, running 33 miles between Manchester and the Calder & Hebble Navigation at Sowerby Bridge. Sadly its heyday was not a long one, and the demise began in 1841 when the Lancashire & Yorkshire Railway was completed. Thus the canals, which themselves had replaced packhorses with far greater efficiency, were quickly ousted by the vastly improved service the railways offered. By 1922 commercial traffic had virtually ceased, and it is only in recent years that a major programme of work has restored this magnificent piece of our history.

• **Hebden Bridge** - please see page 19.

• **Lumbutts** is an attractive settlement nestling in a hollow and dominated by a former water wheel tower. This immense structure originally contained three vertically arranged wheels, fed from above as well as independently. It served a cotton mill that once stood here. Immediately above the tower is Lee Dam, one of three tree-lined dams hovering above the hamlet. It is the scene of an annual New Year 'dip'. Also very prominent is the Top Brink, a sprawling, welcoming hostelry.

Water wheel tower

• **Stoodley Pike** is a major Calderdale landmark. The famous monument was erected in 1815 to celebrate peace after victory over Napoleon, but later collapsed and was replaced in 1856. It stands a mighty 120ft above the 1307ft moortop, and a dark, spiral staircase climbs 39 steps to a viewing balcony. The extensive 360 degree panorama features moorland skylines in almost every direction, while intervening slopes cleverly mask the largely industrialised valley floor.

• **Withens Gate** is the highest point of the run. At the Long Stoop the modern foot traveller's highway, the Pennine Way, meets your centuries old packhorse route known (like several others) as the Long Causeway. The Te Deum Stone's Latin inscription is, translated, We praise thee O Lord!, and being on the summit of the Mankinholes-Withens track is thought to have been used for resting coffins.

• **Mankinholes** is an old handloom weaving settlement by-passed by the 20th century. The great water troughs are a sign of its importance in packhorse days. Most of its visitors today are youth hostellers breaking their Pennine Way journey in the shadow of Stoodley Pike.

START Ogden Water   grid ref. SE 066309
Start at Ogden Water car park, signposted along Ogden Lane
off the A629 Halifax-Keighley road at Causeway Foot.

DISTANCE 7 miles/11km
Off road 5 miles/8km   **On road** 2 miles/3km

TERRAIN Hilly country but a high level start ensures there are
few steep gradients. Some firm tracks, some softer moorland.

ORDNANCE SURVEY MAPS
1:50,000 - Landranger 104, Leeds, Bradford & Harrogate
1:25,000 - Outdoor Leisure 21, South Pennines

REFRESHMENTS
Pubs and tearooms at Ogden. Withens Hotel en route.

S From the car park descend the road past the information centre
and across the dam of **Ogden Water**. In this early section be prepared
for many pedestrians, including young children, on sunny Sundays.
A broad track climbs away outside a plantation. It rises past the trees,
with a golf course on the left and the *Withens Hotel* waiting on the
skyline. Though it presents a lengthy pull to begin with, it is fairly easy
and gets the main climb over with quickly.

At the top the track levels out to reach the pub. At 1391ft above sea
level this is the second highest in West Yorkshire, overtopped only by
the *Buckstones Inn* above Marsden Moor. It was built in 1862 largely
to serve quarrymen. Increasingly featuring in the scene are the great
flapping wind turbines of **Ovenden Moor**. After possible refreshment
turn right along the road. The information site for the windfarm is soon
passed, and the road runs on above Fly Flatts Reservoir (Warley Moor
Reservoir on maps) which is home to a sailing club.

Stoodley Pike is prominent over to the left amidst the Calderdale
moors. This is a long easy section at very high altitude. Other than on
Sundays this road is virtually empty, being no more than a rough track

29

for quite a spell along the top. At the end it begins a long descent towards Oxenhope, with the Haworth and Worth Valley area outspread ahead backed by the Rombalds Moor skyline.

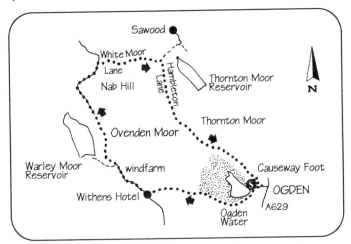

The point to leave it is at the fourth footpath sign on the right (the preceding one being a double one, with a path also signed to the left). Your way is a distinct track known as White Moor Lane. Pass through the gate and at once cross a stream. The track runs on, mostly very easily, becoming Sawood Lane high above Leeming and its reservoir. Up to the right is a prominent cairn on Nab Hill, and the site of many old quarries. At the end a short pull leads up to a wall, which runs a few yards left to a track junction. While the level way goes left, the return route (known as Hambleton Lane) goes through the gate on the right to commence a short climb between old walls. Partly sunken, a brief rougher section is encountered until it eases out.

The crest is quickly gained, a fence left behind, and the wind turbines flap happily again, now on your right. A splendid track runs on through the heather, slowly dropping towards the head of Ogden Clough. Just off route, the head of the clough is a colourful scene featuring some gritstone escarpments. A wall is reached and followed for a while. At a fork remain with the wall, and the track soon becomes enclosed and part sunken between old walls again. As Back Lane it becomes firmer, running on and then down to join Ogden Lane just before reaching the main road.

ALONG THE WAY

• **Ogden Water** is the new name for what was previously the unsung Ogden Reservoir. Built by Halifax Corporation in 1858, the improved access in recent times has made this a very popular venue, featuring woodland paths and an easy circuit of the reservoir. There is an information booth (seasonally manned) and toilets.

• **Ovenden Moor** is a vast tract of unkempt, previously unspoilt moorland reaching the watershed with the gathering grounds of the Worth Valley to the north, itself a side valley of Airedale. Today it is known far and wide however, as the home of the first big windfarm in the district. An information panel and viewing area has been provided, though the few extra yards of path to the viewpoint are largely superfluous for a feature that can be seen from half the county. You will discover that these 23 wind turbines are 100ft high and can power 7,500 homes. Try to calculate how many would be needed to supply Calderdale: you'd certainly need an alternative activity to biking anyway, because there wouldn't be any room left in the outdoors for you and me!

The Causeway Foot Inn, Ogden

LOG OF THE RIDES

No	Date	Start	Finish	Notes
1				
2				
3				
4				
5				
6				

HILLSIDE GUIDES - ACROSS THE NORTH

OTHER BIKING COUNTRY GUIDES
•YORKSHIRE DALES CYCLE WAY   •WEST YORKSHIRE CYCLE WAY
•GLASGOW, Clyde Valley & Loch Lomond
(by Richard Peace)

POCKET RIDES SERIES
•AIRE VALLEY BIKiNG GUIDE   •CALDERDALE BIKING GUIDE
•WHARFEDALE BIKING GUIDE
(by Paul Hannon)
In preparation: •NIDDERDALE BIKING GUIDE

WALKING GUIDES INCLUDE

South Pennines/Lancashire
•BRONTE COUNTRY
•CALDERDALE
•ILKLEY MOOR
•BOWLAND
•PENDLE & THE RIBBLE
•WEST PENNINE MOORS
•SOUTHERN PENNINES

Yorkshire Dales
•HOWGILL FELLS
•THREE PEAKS
•MALHAMDALE
•WHARFEDALE
•NIDDERDALE
•WENSLEYDALE
•SWALEDALE

ALSO
*Lakeland Fells • Peak District • North Pennines • North York Moors
and many Long Distance Paths, including
Coast to Coast Walk • Dales Way • Cleveland Way*

Write for a detailed catalogue and pricelist